This book is presented to

_____

on the occasion of

_____

From

_____

Do to others what you would
have them do to you.
Matthew 7:12

Warriors

Good Manners for a Little Warrior

By Kelly Chapman

Illustrated by Jeff Ebbeler

HARVEST HOUSE PUBLISHERS

EUGENE, OREGON

To my Luke, a boy after God's own heart. The Lord has taught me so much about Himself through you. Your creative and joyful spirit is contagious. May you continue to grow more in love with Jesus every day.

Good Manners for a Little Warrior

Text Copyright © 2011 by Kelly Chapman
Artwork Copyright © 2011 by Jeff Ebbeler

Published by Harvest House Publishers
Eugene, Oregon 97402
www.harvesthousepublishers.com

ISBN 978-0-7369-3724-5

Design and production by Mary pat Design, Westport, Connecticut

Made with nontoxic inks and coatings (CPSIA compliant).

Printed in China

11 12 13 14 15 16 17 18 / **LP** / 10 9 8 7 6 5 4 3 2 1

What is Warrior Prince Academy? For more information, please visit www.royalpurpose.com

Once upon a real time, there lived a boy named Luke. He dreamed of becoming a mighty warrior who would be respected by everyone. But there was a problem. Luke had bad manners, and so did his friends. In fact, they thought manners didn't matter. What do you think?

Let's find out the truth about manners.

Ka-boom!

"What a hit! This play could determine the game!" exclaimed the baseball announcer as the ball headed toward center field.

Luke was too busy playing with the bubble gum he was chewing to notice the ball coming his way...until it was almost too late. He suddenly looked up.

"It looks like it might be a home run!" shouted the announcer. "But wait! Luke Allen is backing up toward the center field fence. He jumps, reaches, and..."

"Ouch! That had to hurt," the announcer said. "Did Luke catch the ball? Is he okay?"

The crowd grew quiet as the baseball coach and medical team ran out to center field. Luke was lying on his back, his mitt against his chest. His eyes were closed and he wasn't moving.

Luke had been totally knocked out cold. While he was on the ground, he began dreaming a royal dream where warriors were courageous, knights were knightly, and castles were majestic. He dreamed that he and his friends were invited to Warrior Prince Academy by a knight who looked exactly like his baseball coach. The knight introduced himself as Sir Britmore.

As they entered the castle, a man ran up to them gasping for air. After he caught his breath, he said, "I'm Constant, the king's royal helper. I have an announcement to make!" He stood straight and tall, took a deep breath.

Hear ye! Hear ye, you hungry bunch!

I have an announcement about your lunch.

This news will surely make you cheer.

The pizzas you ordered are finally here!

"Thank you, Constant," Sir Britmore said. "Boys, we'll continue our warrior prince training after lunch."

"It's about time. We're starving!" shouted the boys as they took off running toward the Royal Banquet Hall, arguing over who would get the first slice.

"I win!" bragged Double as he entered the hall, ran up to the table, and helped himself to a hot slice of pizza. He took a huge bite. "Yikes, that's hot!" he yelled as he quickly spit the food onto a plate. After blowing on the slice in his hand, he gingerly took a nibble.

"Pepperoni is my favorite!" Tomás said as cheese spilled out of his mouth.

"Mine too!" agreed Luke. He reached across Trouble for another slice. "Who wants to see how far I can stretch the cheese on my pizza?" He quickly grabbed some cheese and stretched it as far as it would go.

"Hey, I wanted that slice!" demanded Trouble just before he sneezed all over it.

"Ew, gross!" Luke complained. "You can have it!" He coiled the cheese back on top and slapped the slice on Trouble's plate.

"*Buuurrppp.* That sure was good!" Harris said after he wiped his mouth on his sleeve. "Sir Britmore, do you want some pizza?"

"No, thank you, Harris. I've lost my appetite watching you boys eat. Boys, pay attention," Sir Britmore announced. "Do you know that since you began eating lunch you've committed at least 13 good manners violations? Can anyone tell me what they are?"

The boys looked at each other. They shook their heads.

"Constant, unroll the scroll," ordered Sir Britmore. "Read out loud for the boys the manners violations you wrote down."

Constant unrolled a large scroll, cleared his throat, and began reading...

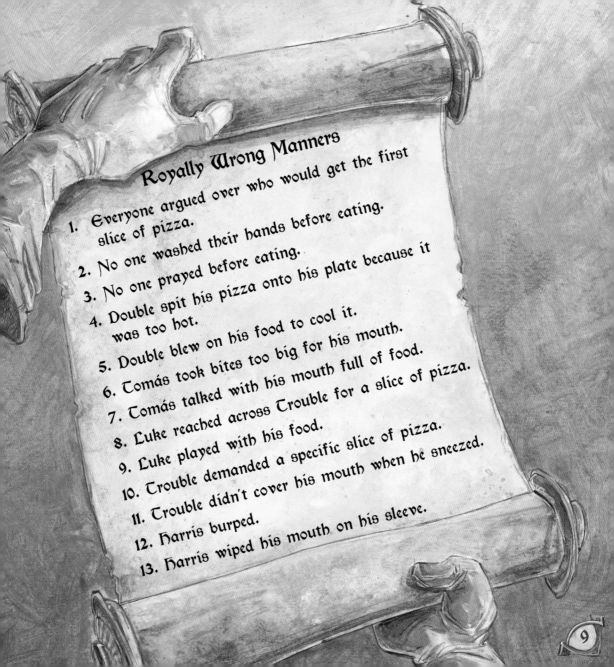

Royally Wrong Manners

1. Everyone argued over who would get the first slice of pizza.

2. No one washed their hands before eating.

3. No one prayed before eating.

4. Double spit his pizza onto his plate because it was too hot.

5. Double blew on his food to cool it.

6. Tomás took bites too big for his mouth.

7. Tomás talked with his mouth full of food.

8. Luke reached across Trouble for a slice of pizza.

9. Luke played with his food.

10. Trouble demanded a specific slice of pizza.

11. Trouble didn't cover his mouth when he sneezed.

12. Harris burped.

13. Harris wiped his mouth on his sleeve.

"Manners? Manners are for girls!" Double declared. "Boys are supposed to be rough, tough, and into messy stuff!"

The other boys nodded in agreement.

"Manners matter for everyone," Sir Britmore asserted. "They show people what's inside our hearts. If we have bad manners, we're showing people that we don't respect them or ourselves. Boys, it's time you learn some good manners. We'll start with Level 1 of 'Manners Matter.' "

"This is going to be so boring," Double whispered to Trouble.

"Yeah, if this gets boring, you'll find me snoring," Trouble rhymed and then laughed.

"Boring did you say?" Sir Britmore cut in. "Do you know that the tradition of shaking hands began hundreds of years ago to prove that a man wasn't carrying a sword or a dagger? If a person wouldn't shake hands, a fight would start. So back then shaking hands meant the difference between life and death. Today, shaking hands is considered good manners to show the other person you're a friend and mean him or her no harm."

"Wow! I didn't know having good manners could save your life!" exclaimed Double. "Tell me more. Uh, I mean, *please* tell me more."

"Now you're talking, Double," Sir Britmore continued. "Let's start with learning how to use the most powerful tool we have."

"Cool! Power tools!" the boys chanted and then gave a cheer.

"Which one are you going to talk about first, Sir Britmore?" Luke asked. "The Bammer Hammer?"

"The Bulldog Jigsaw?" Harris interjected.

"Ha! You guys don't know anything. Everyone, but you, knows it's the 'Big Thrill Cordless Drill,'" Double shouted as he laughed at Luke and Harris.

"That's not right either," Sir Britmore said, shaking his head. "The most powerful tool we have is our words. Using strong words such as 'please' and 'thank you' shows that we respect people. We call these words 'Warrior Prince Power Words.'

"In fact, Double just showed us how *not* to use words. Luke and Harris, how did you feel when Double made fun of you for not knowing the answer?"

"Well, it kind of made me feel bad," confessed Luke.

"It made me feel like I'm not smart," Harris added. "Like I don't know anything."

"That's why it's important we use words to *encourage* people instead of words that discourage people. When we hurt someone with our words—or even our actions—we need to say 'I'm sorry' and then ask the person to forgive us," Sir Britmore said. "We don't want to hurt people. Double, do you have anything you want to say to Luke and Harris?"

13

"Um, I'm sorry for making fun of you," Double said.

"We forgive you," Luke and Harris said at the same time.

Sir Britmore clapped them on their shoulders and said, "Now that you're getting the hang of it, let's see how many Warrior Prince Power Words you all can come up with in ten seconds. Are you ready?" Sir Britmore looked at his watch. "Okay. On your mark, get set, go!"

"You're welcome and excuse me!" shouted Luke.

"Hello and good-bye!" yelled Harris.

"Yes, sir and no, sir!" Double hollered.

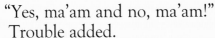

"Yes, ma'am and no, ma'am!"
Trouble added.

"Por favor and gracias!"
Tomás said in Spanish.

"Time's up!" Sir Britmore said. "Wow! You came up with ten power words in ten seconds. That's impressive!

"Boys, I think you're ready to discover the treasure in Level 2 of 'Manners Matter,'" Sir Britmore confided. "But, I have to warn you. If you decide to go to the next level, you'll never be the same. So who's with me? Who is ready for an adventure?"

"Count us in!" Double crowed. "One for all and all for one! Come on, guys! Let's go treasure hunting."

Chapter Three – The Knights Code of Honor

Pleased with the boys' excitement about finding the treasure in good manners, Sir Britmore smiled and said, "Whoa, boys! Not so fast. The key to unlocking this treasure is in the Knights Code of Honor. Who remembers and wants to share the Knights Code of Honor?"

"Oh, I do!" Harris said, raising his hand. He was the brainiac of the bunch. "It's 'Love the Lord your God with all your heart, soul, and mind, and love your neighbor as yourself.'"

"Very good!" Sir Britmore said. "Do you remember when Jesus said that loving God and loving others are the two most important things we are to do? The Knights Code of Honor is from the Bible. It has a lot to say about how we treat others. And that takes us to the key to finding the gold…"

"Quick! Someone get a Bible and see if there's a key in it!" exclaimed Tomás.

"I don't think Sir Britmore is talking about a real key," Luke said thoughtfully. "The kind of key he's talking about is more like a clue. I think…"

"Stop!" interrupted Trouble. "Don't say it out loud, Luke. If you tell Double and me first, it can be our secret and the three of us can share the gold."

"Hey, what happened to 'All for one and one for all'?" Harris admonished.

"Yes! That's not fair," Tomás added as he jumped up from his chair. He moved so fast that his chair fell over and landed on Double's big toe.

"Ouch! Oh, my toe!" Double jumped up and hopped around the room, holding one foot off the floor.

"Uh-oh, I think I'm in double trouble," Tomás groaned.

"You've got that right!" threatened Trouble. "We're not sharing anything with you now!"

"Hey, don't talk to my friend like that!" Luke snarled.

"Boys! Boys! Is this how warrior princes act?" asked Sir Britmore. "Everyone sit down and relax for a minute. Doesn't the Knights Code of Honor mean anything to you?"

Everyone stopped arguing, sat down, and hung their heads. Sir Britmore was right.

Looking up, Luke said, "Sir Britmore, the Knights Code of Honor means everything to us, and we're sorry for breaking it."

The other boys nodded as Luke continued, "As I was going to say, I think the clue to finding the gold is the word 'love.' And we haven't done a very good job of loving one another today."

"Luke's right," Double agreed. "We've been selfish and not acting the way God wants us to act. Please forgive us. We haven't been treating you the way we want you to treat us, and that's wrong."

All the boys nodded and smiled.

"Apologies accepted," Sir Britmore confirmed. "Do you remember when I said that going to the next level would change you? Well, I think it just did."

"But everyone looks the same to me," Tomás said.

"That's because you're looking for a change on the outside, Tomás. I'm talking about a change *inside your hearts*," Sir Britmore explained. "You boys have just discovered the gold in the treasure. It's called the 'Golden Rule'!"

"Is that a ruler that's made out of gold?" asked Double.

"No, it's a truth we get from the Bible. Matthew 7:12 says, 'So in everything, do to others what you would have them do to you,'" answered Sir Britmore. "This valuable treasure means we think of others first. The key to keeping the Golden Rule is following the code of loving God and loving others. When you do, you become a Code Keeper instead of a Code Breaker. The choice is up to you. Which one do you want to be? Let's take a look at the differences."

Code Keeper

Loves God

Loves others

Treats others the way he wants to be treated

Shakes hands, makes eye contact

Respects and shares with everyone

Waits his turn to talk

Takes turns

Shares

Speaks truthfully

Code Breaker

Loves himself and brags

Thinks of himself first

Teases, pushes, and shoves

Keeps hands in pockets, slouches

Whispers to one person in a group

Acts rudely and interrups

Cuts in line

Acts selfishly

Lies

"Sir Britmore, we've all decided to be Code Keepers!" Luke announced.

"Great! Then it's on to Level 3, where we'll put our manners where our mouths are," Sir Britmore chuckled mysteriously.

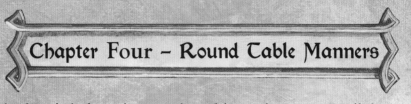

"Constant, the king's helper, has set the table in the Great Hall for our Round Table Manners lesson," Sir Britmore announced.

"Constant must have been in a hurry," said Tomás as he stared at the messy table.

"Actually, he set the table this way for a reason," Sir Britmore explained. "We're going to have a contest to see who can arrange his plate, glass, spoon, fork, knife, and napkin in the right place setting order the fastest. The winner gets to choose dessert. You have two minutes, starting now…"

"Time's up!" Sir Britmore announced after two minutes.

The boys were finished, but not one place setting was done correctly. In fact, the table looked worse than it had when the boys arrived! And Double's place setting looked like the Leaning Tower of Pisa.

"Well, it looks like Burpie gets to choose the dessert since his dog bowl is the only dish in the correct spot," Sir Britmore said. "We need to discover what the correct way is to set a table. Let's call Constant and have him show us where each piece goes."

"How can I help you, Sir Britmore?" Constant asked.

"The boys need some help learning how to set a table."

"I can do that," Constant said, and he began to sing,

> Setting the table can be easy as one, two, three,
> Just follow these steps and you will agree.
> First you take your plate and place it on the table,
> Then top it with your napkin, and fold it if you're able.
> Next place your dinner fork to the left side of your plate,
> With your salad fork by its side as if it were its mate.
> Then gently place your knife by your plate on the right
> To its right side goes your teaspoon that's smaller in height.
> Your glass crowns your plate on the upper-right side,
> Now you can set a table with confidence and pride.

"Okay, boys, you get to try again," Sir Britmore said.

The boys went to work, and soon the table looked nice and neat. Everything was in its proper place.

"That wasn't so hard, thanks to Constant," Luke admitted.

"Now that you know how to set a table, it's time to test your table etiquette, which is another way to say table manners, with the 'Whiz Kid Manners Quiz,'" Sir Britmore announced. "This little test will show how much you know. There are five multiple-choice questions. Circle the answer you think is correct."

(Dear reader, you can take this test along with Luke and the rest of the warrior princes. It can be found at the end of this book.)

24

"Yes! I got a perfect score!" announced Luke.

"So did I! And since I finished first, that makes me the winner!" declared Double.

"I'm the first second winner since I finished second," Trouble announced.

The boys were so busy competing over who was the winner that they didn't notice that Sir Britmore had left the room. When he returned, he was carrying a mysterious long, brown bag.

"Attention!" commanded Sir Britmore.

As the boys swung around to look at him, they stood up straight. The brown bag caught their interest.

Double figured there was a huge "Whiz Kid Manners" trophy in it. After all, he had declared himself the winner. "Sir Britmore, is that *my* trophy for winning?" he asked.

"I'm afraid not. The quiz you just took wasn't meant to be a competition—even though you turned it into one. Level 4 of 'Manners Matter' couldn't come at a more perfect time. This last level will be performed outside. That's where I will reveal what's inside my bag. So let's go!"

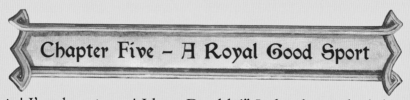

"Yes! I win! I'm the winner! I beat Double!" Luke shouted while jumping up and down.

"Not fair! I wasn't ready," complained Double.

"You were the one who started the race," Luke reminded him.

"Well still, it doesn't count!" Double asserted.

"What counts is having good sportsmanship," Sir Britmore said, interrupting the argument. "That means being polite and kind when playing sports and games. Making excuses about losing and gloating over winning is *not* good sportsmanship. Level 4 is about having good sportsmanship—meaning good manners—on and off the field."

"I thought playing sports was about winning," Luke said.

"Actually it's both. Competing and good manners go together. The Golden Rule of treating others the way you want them to treat you applies to your teammates *and* the members of the opposing teams." Sir Britmore unzipped the brown bag and revealed baseball gloves, baseball bats, baseballs, batters' helmets, and a catcher's protective gear. "One way to practice good sportsmanship is by playing baseball. Who's ready to be a team player?"

"I am! Well, I think I am. What's a team player?" Tomás asked.

"Being a team player means following the coach's directions, playing fair, and encouraging your teammates. It also means treating the opposing team with respect," answered Sir Britmore. "That means not booing them, not calling them names, and not making fun of them. It also means not taunting them by saying you're going to beat them."

"How can we play with only five of us?" observed Harris.

"No need to fear! Boom-Boom Slugger is here!" Constant hollered as he ran up, dressed in a baseball uniform two sizes too small. "At least that's what they called me back in the days when baseball was my game."

"Great! We'll play three on three. Luke, Double, and Trouble will be the home team. Harris, Tomás, and Constant will be the visitors. Visitors, your team bats first. I'll coach and pitch," Sir Britmore said. "Let's play ball!"

Double and Trouble played infield, while Luke played outfield.

Luke was nervous, wondering how he could cover the entire outfield by himself. He decided to chew gum to relax. As soon as the gum got soft, he started pulling it out in long strings and blowing bubbles. Suddenly he heard a loud smack. *Oh oh,* he thought. *That ball was hit hard so it must be coming out here. Where is it?* Luke ran backward, looking up, hoping to see the ball.

Bang! The ball found him.

Wham! His body hit the ground.
His eyes closed as he groaned.

Luke thought he heard someone calling his name, but it sounded like it was a long way off. Finally he cracked open his eyes a bit and looked up. Coach Britmore was standing over him.

"Are you okay?" the coach asked.

Luke noticed all his teammates were gathered around him.

"Manners really do matter," Luke said as he sat up and rubbed his head. "Who knew that playing with your gum could be so dangerous? From now on I'm going to keep my gum inside my mouth and pay attention!" He stood up and stretched.

"Now you're thinking," agreed Coach Britmore. "In fact, I think all of you could use a 'Manners Matter' etiquette class."

"Etiquette? Etiquette is for girls!" complained Double and Trouble.

"No, it's eti*cool*," Luke said. "Sign me up!"

Attention, Little Warrior!

Use the power tools and the royal manners
you've learned as a warrior knight,
and you'll avoid being a jester with all your might!

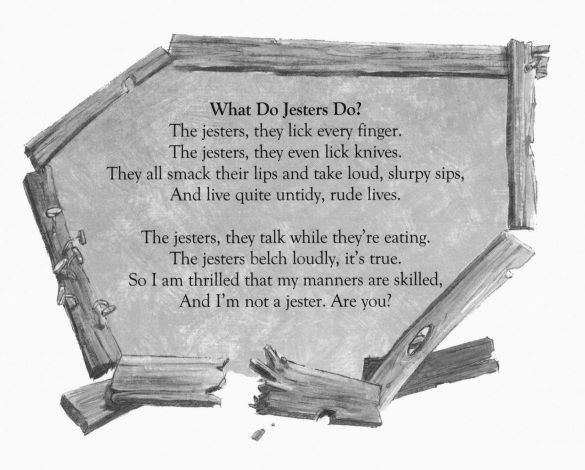

What Do Jesters Do?
The jesters, they lick every finger.
The jesters, they even lick knives.
They all smack their lips and take loud, slurpy sips,
And live quite untidy, rude lives.

The jesters, they talk while they're eating.
The jesters belch loudly, it's true.
So I am thrilled that my manners are skilled,
And I'm not a jester. Are you?

Whiz Kid Manners Quiz

This little test will show how much you know.
There are five multiple-choice questions. Circle the answer you think is correct.

While sitting at the dinner table...

1. What do you do with your napkin?
   a. Whack your brother or sister with it.
   b. Tie it around your neck like a bib.
   c. Place it in your lap.
   d. Who needs a napkin? That's what sleeves are for!

2. When is it okay to place your elbows on the table?
   a. When you're too sleepy to keep your head up.
   b. When you're finished eating.
   c. Right before dessert.
   d. Never.

3. When is it okay to talk with food in your mouth?
   a. Never.
   b. When you have something important to say.
   c. When someone asks you a question.
   d. When you have to laugh at the peas stuck in your brother's nose.

4. What do you do if you have to belch, sneeze, or cough?
   a. You let it all out.
   b. Turn away from the table and cover your mouth with your napkin.
   c. Cover your mouth with your hand, burp, and then continue eating.
   d. Turn to the person next to you and say, "Listen to this!"

5. What do you do when you're finished eating?
   a. Announce you are finished.
   b. Belch, push your plate away, and say, "That was good."
   c. Ask to be excused.
   d. Jump up from the table and go play.

"Let's see how you did," Sir Britmore said. "Let's go over the correct answers.
- For question 1, the correct answer is *c: Place it in your lap.*
- The correct answer for question 2 is *d: Never.*
- The correct answer for question 3 is *a: Never.*
- The correct answer for question 4 is *b: Turn away from the table and cover your mouth with your napkin.*
- The correct answer for question 5 is *c: Ask to be excused.*"